The Elements and Modes

For more on the elements and ɪ

Question 1 • Imagine a busy company that produces the news ... ... channel. You are asked to employ four new people, choosing a suitable job (such as personnel, advertising, line manager, accounts, reporting, production, camera work, etc) for each of them based on the strongest element in their chart.

The first person's chart is strongly Fire, the second heavily Earth, the third is mostly Air, while the fourth has a predominantly Water chart. Which job would you choose for each person, and why? Give your reasons in approximately 50 words for each person.

Question 2 • If someone has a chart with no planets in Air, describe in at least 200 words how you would expect them to behave. For instance, what might their relationships be like? Their friends? Their hobbies? Their work? And how might they compensate for this lack of Air in their horoscope?

Question 3 • Although there are three signs per element (Fire, Earth, Air and Water), each one varies because it has a different mode (Cardinal, Fixed or Mutable). For instance, Aries is Cardinal Fire and Leo is Fixed Fire. This means that each sign in each element has a different method of expression. Bearing this in mind, compile a couple of phrases for each of the twelve signs that would best describe the element/mode combination.

Question 4 • Think of someone you know who embodies the qualities of (a) the Cardinal mode, someone who embodies (b) the Fixed mode, and someone who embodies (c) the Mutable mode. For each person, explain their characteristics in 150 words.

Question 5 •
(i) The Cardinal signs are associated with the ability to get things started. Describe ways in which each of the four Cardinal signs might show their particular type of motivation.
(ii) The Fixed signs are associated with a sense of loyalty. Describe ways in which each of the four Fixed signs might show loyalty and for what reasons.
(iii) The Mutable signs are associated with being communicators and distributors of information. Describe ways in which each of the four Mutable signs might communicate with the rest of the world.
Each of the twelve descriptions should be approximately 50 words.

Question 6 • Mix and match the following descriptions with the correct elements and/ or modes.

(a) A river bursting its banks; (b) Desert; (c) Flood; (d) Mud;
(e) Ice; (f) Solid ground; (g) Steam; (h) Mistral

(i) Fixed Water; (ii) Fire and Water; (iii) Fixed Earth; (iv) Earth and Water;
(v) Fire and Air; (vi) Mutable Water; (vii) Fire and Earth; (viii) Cardinal Water

Question 7 • When assessing a chart, one of the first things to do is to count up the number of planets in each of the different elements and modes. Ignoring the three outer planets, allow one point each for the Sun, Moon, Mercury, Venus, Mars, Jupiter and Saturn, and also include the Ascendant and MC. This gives a total of 9 points.

Here is an example:

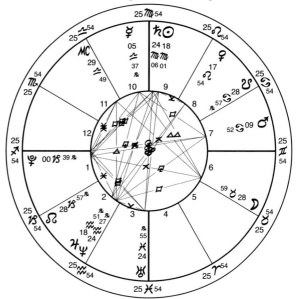

Fire	2
Earth	3
Air	3
Water	1
Cardinal	3
Fixed	3
Mutable	3

Now count up the elements and modes in your own chart.

Write a description, of no less than 100 words, of how you think this combination of elements and modes might be expressed in your own horoscope.

The Signs of the Zodiac

For more information about the signs, see pages 31–74 of *CAH*.

Question 8 • Each one of the following lists of characteristics describes one of the twelve Sun signs. But which goes with which?

(i) Responsible, serious, cautious and pessimistic.
(ii) Analytical, a good eye for detail, nervy and fastidious.
(iii) Indecisive, co-operative, with a need for equality and harmony.
(iv) Motivated, impatient, hot-headed and competitive.
(v) Energetic, honest, clumsy and optimistic.
(vi) Pragmatic, practical, possessive and painstaking.
(vii) Communicative, versatile, changeable and restless.
(viii) Dreamy, idealistic, compassionate, unworldly.
(ix) Proud, dignified, creative and bossy.
(x) Intense, self-willed, suspicious and penetrating.
(xi) Quirky, independent, opinionated and friendly.
(xii) Nurturing, defensive, tenacious and maternal.

Question 9 • The following sentences use a combination of keywords (not necessarily in the right order) to describe two different signs. But which goes with which?

(a) Aries, Sagittarius	i. Someone who plans their holidays meticulously.
(b) Leo, Capricorn	ii. Someone who communicates with charm.
(c) Gemini, Virgo	iii. A person who takes the lead in their friendships.
(d) Cancer, Leo	iv. Someone who needs emotional and material security.
(e) Taurus, Cancer	v. One who resists change in their relationships.
(f) Aries, Aquarius	vi. Someone who is humanitarian and compassionate.
(g) Aquarius, Pisces	vii. A person who is proud of being punctual.
(h) Scorpio, Capricorn	viii. Someone who is private and reserved.
(i) Taurus, Libra	ix. A person who is a secret worrier or fatalist.
(j) Virgo, Sagittarius	x. Someone who enjoys highly detailed gossip.
(k) Scorpio, Pisces	xi. One who expresses themselves through their cooking.
(l) Gemini, Libra	xii. Someone who gets so enthusiastic that they rush into projects without thinking them through first.

Question 10 • The following sentences use a combination of keywords (not necessarily in the right order) to describe three different signs. But which goes with which?

(a) Gemini, Sagittarius, Capricorn	(e) Taurus, Virgo, Pisces
(b) Cancer, Virgo, Sagittarius	(f) Cancer, Libra, Aquarius
(c) Taurus, Libra, Capricorn	(g) Gemini, Leo, Scorpio
(d) Aries, Leo, Aquarius	(h) Aries, Scorpio, Pisces

i. Someone who works at finding a balance between their need for freedom and their need for emotional closeness.

ii. One who chooses conventional and reliable partners.

iii. A person who flamboyantly shows their individuality and competitiveness.

iv. Someone whose strong sense of service and practicality turns them into a martyr.

v. One who fights behind the scenes for charitable causes.

vi. Someone who writes about the financial centres of foreign countries.

vii. A person who is suspicious of people's versatility and success.

viii. Someone who is critical and tactless when on the defensive.

Question 11 • For each of the twelve signs, think of a character (fictional or real) from film, literature or television that you feel personifies the essence of that sign. Give your reasons for each choice in 50 words.

Question 12 • Following the style of the definitions in Question 3, write a sentence describing someone whose qualities match each set of the following three signs:

(a) Cancer, Leo, Pisces	(e) Aries, Leo, Sagittarius
(b) Gemini, Virgo, Aquarius	(f) Taurus, Sagittarius, Aquarius
(c) Aries, Taurus, Libra	(g) Gemini, Cancer, Pisces
(d) Virgo, Scorpio, Capricorn	(h) Libra, Scorpio, Capricorn

Question 13 • Some signs have more in common than others. What links can you see between each of the following pairs of signs? In no less than 100 words for each pair, consider their planetary rulers, elements and modes, as well as their characteristics.

(a) Aries and Sagittarius; (b) Taurus and Libra; (c) Gemini and Virgo; (d) Cancer and Leo; (e) Virgo and Pisces

Question 14 • Thinking about the characteristics of each sign, with its particular set of strengths and weaknesses, choose what you consider to be an ideal job for each of the twelve signs. Give your reasons for each choice in approximately 50 words.

Question 15 • Choose five countries and decide which sign (or signs) you think best embody each country. Give your reasons for each choice in approximately 50 words.

Question 16 • Each sign rules a specific area of the body. State which sign relates to each of the following body parts: (a) stomach; (b) breasts; (c) neck; (d) bowels; (e) feet; (f) spine; (g) kidneys; (h) knees; (i) thighs; (j) head; (k) hands; (l) ankles.

Question 17 • An emphasis on a particular sign indicates certain characteristics. In which signs will the following characteristics be manifested? In some cases, you may decide to choose more than one sign: (a) conservative; (b) escapist; (c) loyal; (d) fair; (e) headstrong; (f) gossipy; (g) modest; (h) practical; (i) tenacious; (j) strong-willed; (k) gregarious; (l) innovative.

The Planets

For more information about the planets, see pages 75–218 of *CAH*.

Question 18 • List both the traditional and modern (where appropriate) planetary ruler(s) for each of the zodiac signs.

Question 19 • Write a short description (up to 100 words each) of the sense of identity, life purpose and goals of someone with the Sun in each of the following signs: (a) Taurus; (b) Cancer; (c) Scorpio; (d) Aquarius.

Question 20 • The transiting Moon is the fastest moving planet in the horoscope.
(i) On average, how long does it spend in each sign?
(ii) Approximately how long does the Moon take to move 1 degree?
(iii) How many days are there from one new moon to the next?

Question 21 • Write a short description of the basic needs and habits of someone with the Moon in each of the following elements: (a) Fire; (b) Earth; (c) Air; (d) Water.

Question 22 •
(i) Thinking about the ways in which Mercury influences our attitudes to learning, our abilities to communicate and our intellectual orientation, write a description of Mercury in each of the following signs: (a) Aries; (b) Leo; (c) Capricorn; (d) Aquarius. Answers should be 100 words for each placement.
(ii) In about 100 words, what do you consider to be the major differences between the Gemini side of Mercury and the Virgo side?

Question 23 • Consider the differences in personal expression and intellectual interests between someone with the Sun in Aries who has (a) Mercury in Pisces; (b) Mercury in Aries; (c) Mercury in Taurus. Allow approximately 100 words for each combination.

Question 24 • What sort of events would you expect to read about in the news under a Mercury retrograde, and what might you expect in your own personal and professional sphere at this time? Your answer should be approximately 200 words.

Question 25 • Considering the ways in which Venus influences our pleasures, tastes, values and styles of relating, write a description of Venus in each of the following signs: (a) Gemini; (b) Cancer; (c) Scorpio; (d) Sagittarius. Answers should be 100 words each.

Question 26 • In about 100 words, what do you consider to be the major differences between the Taurus side of Venus and the Libra side?

Question 27 • Both the Moon and Mercury are linked to types of communication and writing. Consider five ways in which they differ in these areas.

Question 28 • Both the Moon and Venus represent different aspects of the feminine part of our personality. List five typical ways in which the Moon typically represents the feminine aspect of our personality, and five ways in which Venus does.

Question 29 •
(i) How long, on average, does Mars spend in each sign?
(ii) Thinking about the ways in which Mars influences our motivations, drive, aggression and energy, write a 100-word description of Mars in each of the following signs: (a) Taurus; (b) Virgo; (c) Libra; (d) Pisces.
(iii) Which sign placement for Mars would you associate with each of the following: (a) family rows; (b) coming first in an athletics event; (c) becoming successful through your own efforts; (d) visiting somewhere hot and dangerous.

Question 30 • In about 100 words, what do you consider to be the major differences between the Aries side of Mars and the Scorpio side?

Question 31 •
(i) Choose a city or town that you know well and which you think embodies the characteristics of Mercury. Give your reasons in approximately 50 words.
(ii) Now do the same, in 50 words each, with cities or towns that you associate with each of the following planets: (a) Moon; (b) Venus; (c) Mars.

Question 32 •
(i) Choose a famous person who epitomizes Venus and give your reasoning in about 100 words.
(ii) Now do the same for the following planets: (a) Moon; (b) Mercury; (c) Mars. Allow 100 words for each planet.

Question 33 • In about 100 words, what do you consider to be the major differences between the Sagittarius side of Jupiter and the Pisces side?

Question 34 • With reference to convictions, beliefs, philosophy and the urge to find inspiration and meaning, write a short description (approximately 50 words) of Jupiter in each of the following signs: (a) Gemini; (b) Virgo; (c) Libra; (d) Sagittarius.

Question 35 • In about 100 words, what sort of events reported in the news would you associate with Jupiter?

Question 36 •
(i) Roughly how long does it take Saturn to return to its natal position in a chart?
(ii) What sort of events would you expect when this happens?
(iii) Which events happened at this time to you (or to a loved one if you aren't old enough to have experienced your Saturn return)? How do these reflect the sign or house position of your natal Saturn, or its planetary aspects? Give the appropriate significators within your answer.

Question 37 • Some planets have a lot in common while others have many differences. List 10 ways in which the following differ from one another: (a) Jupiter and Saturn; (b) Saturn and Uranus; (c) Neptune and Pluto.

Question 38 •
(i) List a few key phrases associated with Jupiter and Saturn when they are in aspect to each other in a horoscope.
(ii) How often do transiting Jupiter and Saturn form a conjunction?

Question 39 • List six professions you associate with each of the following planets: (a) Saturn; (b) Jupiter; (c) Mars. Give a brief explanation of your choices.

Question 40 • On page 182 of *The Contemporary Astrologer's Handbook*, Sue Tompkins states that, over time, Uranian things turn into Saturn. Give three examples of how this has happened in history, e.g. politically, technologically or with trends.

Question 41 • Assign a planet to each of the following: sugar; reduction; school; university; experience; silver; gold; erratic; long-distance travel; fertilizer; assertion; values; the urge to merge; Hollywood; duty; telephone; slow; perfume; clock; revolution; oblivion; brother; notepad; bowl; gun; heart; security; decoration; watercolour painting; anger; history; blackmail; mother; uncle; quizzes.

Question 42 •
(i) If you meet someone who has trouble saying 'no' to an extra glass of wine, can't resist buying pairs of beautiful shoes, enjoys reading fairytales and works as an aromatherapist, which planet would you expect to be strong in their chart?
(ii) If you meet someone who doesn't suffer fools gladly, who is erratic and unconventional, and who has a strongly idealistic streak, which planet would you expect to be strong in their chart?
(iii) If you meet someone who loves wearing silver jewellery, who is moody, defensive and enjoys cooking, which planet would you expect to be strong in their chart?

Question 43 • Imagine that the following planets are invited to a party. Describe in approximately 100 words for each planet: how each of them would dress, their reasons for attending, how they would behave on arrival, how they would interact with others and how they would attempt to enjoy themselves. The planets are: (a) Moon; (b) Venus; (c) Jupiter; (d) Saturn; (e) Neptune.

Question 44 • Each of the phrases numbered i to ix conjures up thoughts of a particular planet. But which one? The phrases numbered x to xv involve two planets. Can you identify each pair?

(i) Always look on the bright side of life

(ii) It never rains but it pours

(iii) Always expect the unexpected

(iv) Seeing red

(v) As sweet as sugar

(x) Thunder and lightning

(xi) As black as coal

(xii) A born writer

(vi) Out of the frying pan into the fire

(vii) Paradise

(viii) Right on time

(ix) A bolt from the blue

(xiii) On hot coals

(xiv) My brother's keeper

(xv) Fairytale romance

Question 45 • What sort of presents would you buy someone who had the following planets strongly placed in their horoscope: (a) Venus; (b) Neptune; (c) Jupiter; (d) Mercury. Give your reasons for each choice.

Aspects and Planetary Combinations

For more on aspects and planetary combinations, see pages 219–244 of *CAH*.

Question 46 •

(i) List the five major (Ptolemaic) aspects, with the number of degrees of orb that are generally suggested for each one. Describe how each aspect manifests.

(ii) Choose four minor aspects and give the number of degrees of orb that are suggested for each one. Describe how each aspect manifests in a natal chart.

Question 47 • Here are the charts of three world leaders. Allow 200 words for each part of each section. (You may wish to do some biographical research before answering.)

(i) Each of them has a planet rising: Adolf Hitler has Uranus rising in Libra; Tony Blair has Mars rising in Gemini; and George W Bush has Mercury–Pluto rising in Leo. How has each of these Ascendant pictures been demonstrated in the personality and how they view life?

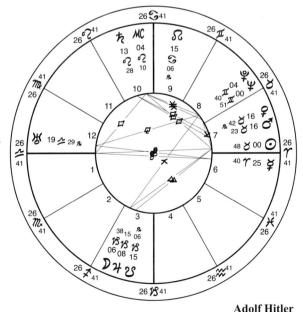

Adolf Hitler

(ii) Both George W Bush and Adolf Hitler have the Moon conjunct Jupiter, although in different signs. How has this aspect manifested in their lives?

(iii) All three men have major aspects to their Suns. Tony Blair has the Sun square Pluto; Adolf Hitler has the Sun and Mercury conjunct his Descendant; and George Bush has the Sun square Moon–Jupiter and Neptune. Describe some of the ways that these aspects have affected their life path and their relationship with their father.

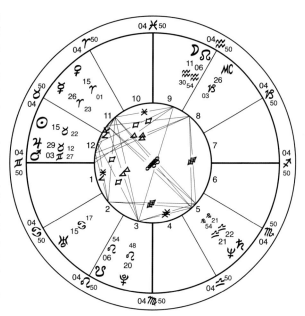

Tony Blair

(iv) Take a look at their Saturns. For George Bush, the only aspect his Saturn makes is a square to his MC/IC axis, thereby creating a T-square. How has this affected him? How does he express this aspect? Adolf Hitler has Venus and Mars square Saturn. How did he express this? Tony Blair has Venus and Mercury opposite Saturn and Neptune. Give some examples of the ways these aspects have played out in his life.

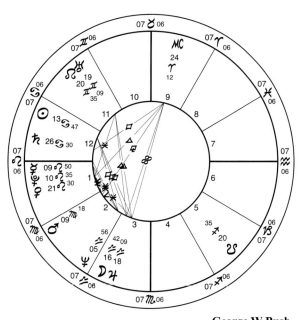

George W Bush

Question 48 • Sometimes aspects form a particular pattern. But what do they mean?
(i) What is a T-square and how would you expect it to operate in a horoscope?
(ii) What is a Grand Cross and how would you expect it to operate in a horoscope?
(iii) What are the differences in expression between a Fixed Grand Cross and a Cardinal Grand Cross?

Question 49 • Consider someone with Venus square Mars in their horoscope. In approximately 200 words, how would you expect them to behave in the bedroom, in the boardroom and on the first day of the January sales?

Question 50 • Consider this mind map of the Sun in aspect to Neptune. Using a similar format, please do the same for the Sun in aspect to Uranus.

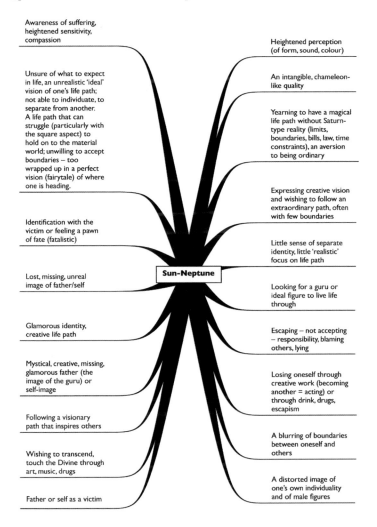

Question 51 • Compose 12 to 15 phrases on the following planetary combinations (lettered a–f), keeping the following example of Mercury–Saturn phrases in mind:

- precise thinking
- the disciplined mind
- serious-minded
- thorough ideas and preparation
- talking about experience
- respected for knowledge
- (eventually becoming) the voice of authority

- fear of academic failure
- narrow-minded
- fear of sounding stupid
- learning the hard way
- language or learning difficulties
- afraid to express opinions
- negative thinking

(a) Mars–Saturn
(b) Moon–Jupiter
(c) Venus–Neptune

(d) Venus–Uranus
(e) Sun–Pluto
(f) Mercury–Uranus

Question 52 • What sort of outfit do you think someone might choose to wear to a fancy dress party if they had the following planetary combinations strongly placed in their chart: (a) Moon–Venus; (b) Moon–Pluto; (c) Sun–Jupiter; (d) Mars–Uranus. Give your reasons for each choice in approximately 50 words.

Question 53 • What sort of social, political or geophysical events would you associate with the following planets: (a) Saturn; (b) Uranus; (c) Neptune; (d) Pluto. Give your reasons for each choice in approximately 50 words.

Question 54 • What sort of sweets or chocolates would you buy for someone with each of the following planetary combinations: (a) Moon–Saturn; (b) Moon–Venus; (c) Moon–Neptune; (d) Moon–Pluto.

Question 55 • In approximately 200 words, consider how your own Sun, Moon and Ascendant sign (if known) complement and/or conflict with one another.

Question 56 • How would someone dress, and what would be their personal style in clothing, if they had the following planetary combinations conjunct their Ascendant: (a) Mars–Pluto; (b) Sun–Venus; (c) Sun–Saturn; (d) Moon–Uranus. Give your reasons for each choice in approximately 50 words.

Question 57 • How does the influence of Uranus vary in each of the following planetary combinations in a natal chart: (a) Sun–Uranus; (b) Moon–Uranus; (c) Mercury–Uranus; (d) Venus–Uranus; (e) Mars–Uranus. Allow approximately 100 words for each combination.

Question 58 • When two planets are connected in an angular relationship, the energies of the two planets will be affected by the specific aspect that links them. List some of the differences between each of the following sets of aspects:

(a) Sun conjunct Uranus and Sun square Uranus
(b) Venus sextile Pluto and Venus opposition Pluto
(c) Moon trine Mars and Moon conjunct Mars
(d) Mercury square Neptune and Mercury opposition Neptune
(e) Moon sextile Jupiter and Moon conjunct Jupiter

Question 59 • What sort of films on DVD would you buy for someone who had a major aspect between the following planets in their horoscope: (a) Mercury–Uranus; (b) Moon–Mars; (c) Venus–Neptune; (d) Mars–Saturn. Give your reasons for each choice.

Question 60 • You're planning a special party but can't decide which of four different dates to choose, so you consult your ephemeris.
   (i) How do you think the party would turn out, based on each of the following major aspects for that day: (a) Sun square Saturn; (b) Venus conjunct Jupiter; (c) Moon opposition Uranus; (d) Mercury trine Mars.
   (ii) Which planetary aspect (from any combination) would you choose for your own birthday party, and why?

Question 61 • Imagine that you run a dating agency that uses astrology as a guide to the sort of partner someone is looking for. Describe in approximately 50 words the sort of partner you would choose for someone with each of the following planetary combinations: (a) Sun–Moon; (b) Mercury–Venus; (c) Venus–Uranus; (d) Mars–Neptune.

Question 62 • What sort of events would you associate with the following:
   (a) An opposition from transiting Uranus.   (c) A trine from transiting Jupiter.
   (b) A sextile by transit to Mercury.   (d) A square from transiting Mars.

Question 63 • What conclusions would you draw about a person's character if a particular aspect were completely missing: (a) trines; (b) squares; (c) oppositions.

Question 64 • What sort of pet (use your imagination – it can be as ordinary or exotic as you like) do you think might appeal to someone with the following planetary combinations strong in their chart: (a) Sun–Moon; (b) Sun–Pluto; (c) Mercury–Uranus; (d) Venus–Mars. Give reasons for each of your choices.

Question 65 • Which skills would you associate with the following combinations, and how do you think they might be useful in the workplace: (a) Mercury–Mars; (b) Mercury–Jupiter; (c) Mercury–Saturn; (d) Mercury–Pluto. Give your reasons for each choice.

Question 66 • Teenagers often go through a spell of what their parents regard as bad behaviour, in which they rebel against their upbringing, test the boundaries of their relationship with their parents and start expressing their adult selves. What sort of behaviour would you expect to see in teenagers with the each of the following combinations: (a) Venus–Mars; (b) Venus–Jupiter; (c) Mercury–Neptune; (d) Moon–Pluto.

The Houses

For more information about the houses, see pages 245–301 of *CAH* and pages 31–112 and 285–9 of *TH*.

Question 67 • Each of the 12 houses rules a particular sphere of life. Assign one house to each of the following: (a) creativity; (b) relationships; (c) shared resources; (d) values and priorities; (e) open challenges; (f) personal appearance; (g) home and roots; (h) status; (i) siblings and neighbours; (j) private fears; (k) health; (l) friends.

Question 68 • The houses are divided into three groups: angular, succedent and cadent. What role does each set of houses (angular; succedent; cadent) play in the horoscope? Your answer should be approximately 150 words in length.

Question 69 • Assign a house to each of the following: funeral directors; work conditions; hospitals; roads; the future; personal finances; royalty; fear; short journeys; pets; family roots; spirituality; hobbies; ambitions; mannerisms; show business; kitchen; charities; prison; prizes; public enemies; school playground; monasteries; bureaucratic organizations; courts of law; sports ground; youth club; neighbourhood.

Question 70 • In this birth chart, all the planets except for Neptune are confined within two quadrants. What does each of these quadrants represent, and how do you imagine this emphasis might affect the person as they go through their life? The chart has been calculated in the Placidus system to clearly identify the four quadrants.

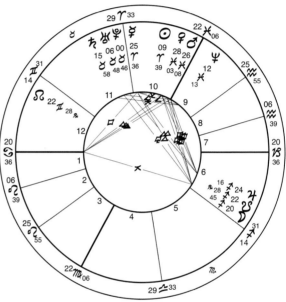

Vincent Van Gogh (Placidus Houses)

Question 71 • A conjunction of planets has a particular set of associations that will be channelled into a specific area of life according to its house position. For instance, someone with Mars conjunct Jupiter (enormous stamina, great competitive instinct) in the 5th could excel at sports or games, whereas someone with the conjunction in the 11th might belong to a running club or have friends who are very sporty.

Describe how you think a Venus–Uranus conjunction might be expressed when it falls in each of the following: (a) 1st house; (b) 5th house; (c) 7th house; (d) 12th house.

Question 72 • The house position of a planet will always affect how that planet is expressed in the horoscope. Describe the differences between the following placements.

(a) Saturn in the 1st and 10th house
(b) Moon in the 2nd and 8th house
(c) Venus in the 4th and 11th house
(d) Jupiter in the 6th and 3rd house
(e) Uranus in the 12th and 5th house
(f) Pluto in the 7th and 9th house

Question 73 • A house is not only governed by the sign on the cusp of that house, but is also influenced by any other sign fully contained within that house. This means that some houses are affected by at least two signs, if not more (with an unequal house system).

Analysing the sign on the cusp of each house will give you information about that house, but you will gain even more insight if you study the planetary ruler of the sign on the cusp and this planet's position in the horoscope. For instance, if a house is ruled by Leo, its planetary ruler is the Sun. Finding the Sun in the horoscope, and noting its house position, sign and aspects, will give you additional information about the Leo-cusped house.

Working with the horoscope on the right, write down a list of (a)

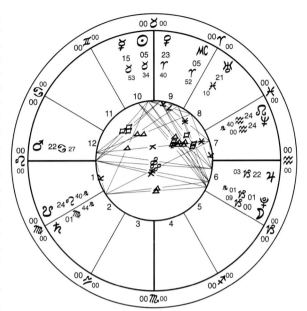

the signs on each house cusp; (b) the planetary ruler(s) of those signs, and (c) the house position of the planetary ruler(s) of those signs. For example, the 1st house: (a)Leo; (b) the Sun; (c) the Sun is in the 10th house. Put simply, the ruler of the 1st house (Ascendant) is in the 10th house (linking both houses), or you may wish to write: the ruler of the 1st house is the Sun in Taurus in the 10th house.

Question 74 • The planet ruling the sign on the cusp of a house provides additional information about how that house operates. For instance, when someone has the ruler of the 1st house in the 2nd house, their appearance (1st house) might make money (2nd house) for them. Describe (in no less than 50 words for each) how you might expect the following combinations of houses to manifest:

(i) Ruler of the 7th house in the 2nd
(ii) Ruler of the 3rd house in the 12th
(iii) Ruler of the 8th house in the 8th
(iv) Ruler of the 4th house in the 10th

(v) Ruler of the 11th house in the 10th
(vi) Ruler of the 9th house in the 6th
(vii) Ruler of the 5th house in the 1st
(viii) Ruler of the 2nd house in the 5th

Putting it All Together

For more information about this section, see pages 313–19 of *CAH* and pages 113–126 of *TH*.

Question 75 • There are twelve different Ascendant–Descendant (e.g. Aries Asc, Libra Desc; Libra Asc, Aries Desc) combinations. Write a sentence to describe some of the major relationship issues experienced by each pair.

Question 76 • There are twelve different MC–IC combinations (e.g. Taurus MC and Scorpio IC; Scorpio MC and Taurus IC). Write a sentence to describe some of the major issues from the early family life (IC) that would affect their role in society, their ambitions and their professional strivings in the world (MC).

Question 77 • Two of your friends were born with the Sun in Taurus. One of them has the Moon in Pisces, and the other has the Moon in Capricorn. What are the differences between the two pairs of planets: (a) Sun in Taurus, Moon in Pisces; (b) Sun in Taurus, Moon in Capricorn.

Question 78 • In terms of identity and personal needs, how would a woman with the Sun in Virgo and the Moon in Aquarius differ from a woman with the reverse combination of the Sun in Aquarius and the Moon in Virgo? Allow approximately 200 words in total.

Question 79 • In terms of relationship expectations, attraction and sexual desire, how would a man with Venus in Pisces and Mars in Aries differ from a man with the reverse combination of Venus in Aries and Mars in Pisces? Allow 200 words in total.

Question 80 •
(i) Consider each of the ten planets and their possible connection(s) to religion, faith and belief. Which planet(s) would you associate with the following: (a) the media evangelist (televangelist); (b) the atheist; (c) the religious zealot or crusader; (d) daily practice; (e) prayer; (f) confession; (g) meditation; (h) belief in a higher power; (i) the abuse of power in religion; (j) cults. Briefly explain your reasons.
(ii) Which planets would you associate with specific religions? Allow 400 words.

Question 81 • Imagine that this man will be coming to you for a reading to mark his 21st birthday. Please note that his time of birth may be an approximation.

(i) First, take note of the balance of elements and modes in his chart. Which are the strongest and which are the weakest? What does this immediately tell you about him?

(ii) Look at the way the planets are arranged in the chart. What is the name of this pattern and how might you expect it to work out in his life?

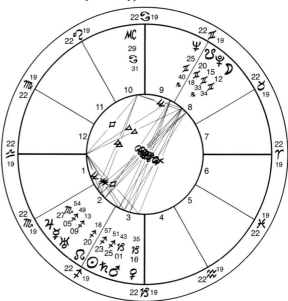

He wants guidance in the following areas:

(iii) His career. Where do you think his talents might lie? How can he make the best of them?

(iv) His relationship with his parents (both still alive at the time of the consultation). Do you think this is a happy or successful relationship? Does he have a stronger relationship with one parent? If so, which one and why?

(v) His finances. What is his attitude to money? Would you expect him to become wealthy or do you think he will always struggle to make a living for himself?

(vi) Study his 10th house. What does it tell you? Is this someone you expect to be in the spotlight during his life or do you expect him to keep a low profile?

(vii) Follow the trail of the dispositor of his Ascendant until it reaches what is known as the final dispositor. It runs like this: Libra Ascendant ruled by Venus in Capricorn; Saturn (ruler of Capricorn) in Sagittarius; Jupiter (ruler of Sagittarius) in Scorpio; Pluto (ruler of Scorpio) in Gemini; Mercury (ruler of Gemini) in Sagittarius. This means that Mercury is the final dispositor of this man's Ascendant because Jupiter has already appeared in this trail, so cannot appear again. His Libran Ascendant is therefore flavoured by his Mercury in Sagittarius in the 2nd house. If you combine the two, what do you think this might say about him?

Question 82 • This is the chart of Ted Turner, the American tycoon who was the founder of the cable company CNN as well as several other media companies. He is one of the men who has changed the way we watch the news – which may or may not be a good thing. He is still worth billions of dollars, despite having been fired from the board of his company in 2000.

When answering the following questions, give as much information as possible, complete with significators.

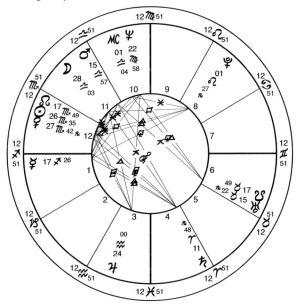

Ted Turner

(i) Where do you think his money-making talents lie in his chart?

(ii) Where can you see the abilities that made him one of the most influential media tycoons of the 20th century?

(iii) What is the final dispositor of his MC and what does it suggest about him?

(iv) He is famously outspoken and controversial, and one of his nicknames is 'Mouth of the South'. Where can you see this outspokenness?

(v) His third wife was the actress, political activist and fitness guru Jane Fonda (21 December 1937, 09.14 EST, Manhattan, NY, USA. Source: birth certificate). Show the ways in which she is described so vividly in Ted Turner's chart.

Question 83 • Margaret Thatcher became Britain's first woman Prime Minister in 1979, a position that she held until she resigned in November 1990. She had come a long way from her origins in Grantham, and was taught to lower the pitch of her voice to make herself sound more authoritative. She married Denis Thatcher in 1951 and their twins, Mark and Carol, were born in Chelsea, London on 15 August 1953 at 14.50 and 14.52 respectively (source: birth certificates).

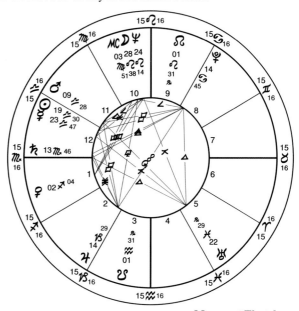

Margaret Thatcher

(i) We know a lot about her as a politician, and that she was famously called 'The Iron Lady', but what does her chart tell you about her life as a mother?

(ii) Her political career would have interfered with her duties as the mother of two young children. How do you think she felt about that?

(iii) Do you think her relationship with her children is clear-cut or do you think there is room for confusion? Give your answers with plenty of astrological significators.

(iv) Where would you see her Government's conflict with the miners and the IRA?

Question 84 • Rock music has attracted performers who thrive on controversy and shock tactics. One of them is Marilyn Manson, the self-styled 'Antichrist Superstar' who has cultivated a satanic, anti-parental persona. In the past he has decorated the stage with skinned goats' heads. Not the ideal man for a girl to bring home to meet her mother...

(i) Study his Mercury by sign, house and aspect. He has said that he is 'exploring the limits of censorship'. Describe all the ways you can see this in his Mercury.

(ii) Where in his chart can you see his outrageous image?

(iv) Manson had quite a conventional upbringing but it had its difficulties. He has said: 'My father had a very violent temper, and he was never home, so I was kind of a mama's boy. But I had a weird relationship with my mom as a kid because it was kind of abusive – but on my part. I wish I could go back and change the way I treated my mom because I used to be really rude to her, and she didn't really have any kind of control over me.' Where could this be seen?

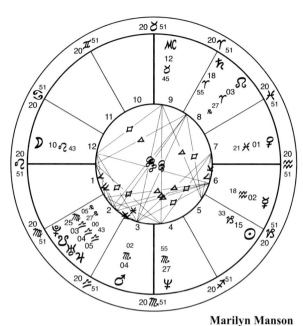

Marilyn Manson

(iii) How do you interpret the 'softer' placement of Venus in Pisces square Neptune?

Question 85 • As soon as she hit the TV screens on *Britain's Got Talent*, and YouTube, on 11 April 2009, the year belonged to Susan Boyle. Much was made of her ungroomed appearance, which was such a contrast with that of the judges, and there were many stories of viewers being moved by the purity of her voice. Her first album, released on 24 November 2009, quickly sold millions.

(i) She has a Cardinal T-square with the Sun opposite Moon, both square Mars. How does she express this?

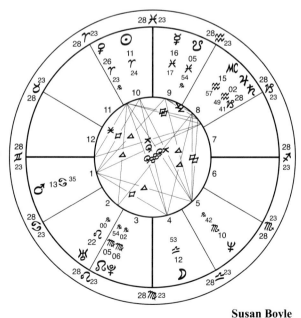

Susan Boyle

(ii) Venus in Aries is the final dispositor of her Aquarian MC. Looking at the house position, sign and aspects of Venus, how has it influenced her public persona?

(iii) There has been a lot of publicity about her alleged erratic behaviour, inability to withstand the pressure of the celebrity bubble in which she finds herself, and her brief spells in psychiatric clinics. Yet when she performs she commands the stage and brims with confidence. How does her emotional instability show up in her chart? And where can you see her confidence as a performer?

Question 86 • The first episode of the television show *Friends* was filmed before a live audience in Burbank, California, and screened throughout the US. It was a fast-paced comedy centred on six 20-something singleton friends living in each other's pockets in New York. *Friends* was a huge hit, with a major cultural influence on everything from Rachel's hairstyle (known to all hairdressers as 'a Rachel') to the rise of the coffee house culture. During its 10 seasons it was nominated for over 60 Primetime Emmy Awards. Here is the chart for the start of that first episode.

(i) At least one planet is conjunct each angle. Interpret each in turn.

(ii) Where in the chart can you see the significators that describe the show – a comedy in which the lives of six friends are closely intertwined.

(iii) The show ran for ten seasons. Where in the chart can you see evidence that it would last so long?

(iv) Before salary negotiations began for the third season, the six actors agreed to negotiate collectively so they would all receive the same amount of money. This arrangement continued for the rest of the life of the show. Where can you see this all-for-one-and-one-for-all attitude in the chart?

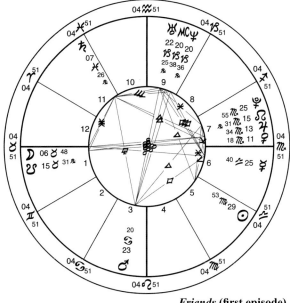

Friends **(first episode)**

Question 87 • Arnold Schwarzenegger is a towering presence in more ways than one. He follows in the tradition of a small but select band of actors who have successfully switched from Hollywood to American politics. At the time of writing, he is the Governor of California, having been elected to the position in October 2003.

(i) He has had three successful careers to date: he was a Guinness World Record body builder; then he became a major Hollywood star; and now he is a successful politician.

Where can you see this versatility?

(ii) When he stood for the governorship he said he had no need to accept campaign donations because he had plenty of money of his own. Where might the fact that he is a self-made millionaire be shown?

(iii) His wife is Maria Shriver, who belongs to the Kennedy family. Where can you see this link to such an important political dynasty in Schwarzenegger's chart?

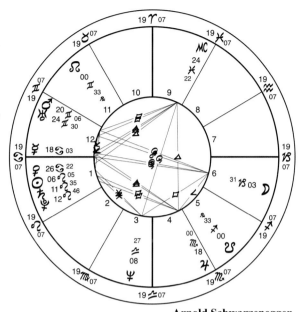

Arnold Schwarzenegger

Question 88 • Grace Kelly is another member of the acting profession who later became famous in an entirely different sphere. She was the toast of Hollywood, having made several very successful films, when she met Prince Rainier III of Monaco in April 1955. They were married, in a fairytale wedding, a year later, when she was 26. There had been pressure on Prince Rainier to marry, because if he didn't produce an heir his principality would revert to French control. Like another beautiful blonde who later married a prince, Princess Grace (as she became on her marriage) found that life in a gilded royal cage didn't necessarily mean being happy ever after.

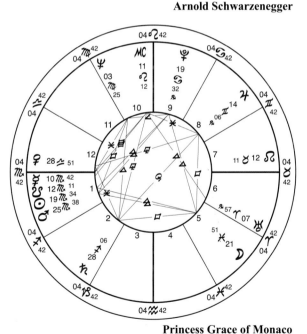

Princess Grace of Monaco

(i) Grace Kelly was one of the most glamorous Hollywood actresses of her generation. She had class, style, a cool beauty and came from a wealthy background. Where are these characteristics shown in her chart?

(ii) After her marriage, Prince Rainier insisted that she retire from Hollywood, even to the point of banning the screening of her films. She had three children and became involved in many charities. She later said that her marriage was like a prison. Where can you see this sense of marital imprisonment in her chart?

(iii) Alfred Hitchcock always preferred blonde leading ladies for his thrillers, saying they were 'a symbol of the heroine' and that the audience would be more suspicious of brunettes. Many of the blondes were depicted as perfect, aloof, ice goddesses whose outer coolness hides a red-hot inner fire. Grace Kelly herself was one of Hitchcock's favourite leading ladies. Can you see why?

Question 89 • David Tennant was the tenth actor to play the iconic Time Lord Doctor Who in the series of the same name. It was the fulfilment of a lifelong ambition: when he was three he told his parents that he wanted to become an actor so he could play Doctor Who. His performance was credited with helping to revive interest in the show, which had been off the television screens for 14 years.

(i) Where in his chart can you see the significators for his role as Doctor Who?

(ii) Before taking over as the new Doctor in *Doctor Who*, he had successfully appeared on television as Casanova in a drama series about the 18th-century Italian sexual adventurer. Casanova, who is often described as 'the world's greatest lover', was a poorly educated man who moved in the grandest European circles and is best known for his memoirs that recount

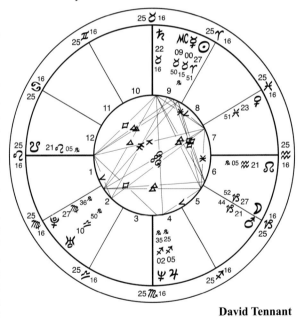

David Tennant

so many of his sexual encounters. Where can you see the significators for Casanova's character in Tennant's chart?

(iii) Although David Tennant normally speaks with a Scottish accent, he is adept at many different accents. His Doctor Who was distinctly English. Where in his chart can you see this ability to use a variety of accents?

Question 90 • Love her or hate her, there's no denying that singer–dancer Britney Spears has had a massive impact on the pop industry since her first smash hit album in 1999. She's been a performer since her early childhood, and was taking part in commercials while still at junior school. So far, her life has been far from that of an ordinary American girl.

After a 'joke' wedding to an old friend in January 2004 (the marriage was annulled a day later) she married Kevin Federline on 18 September 2004 and they had two boys:

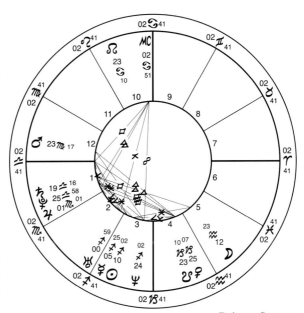

Britney Spears

Sean was born on 14 September 2005 and Sutton was born on 12 September 2006. Britney filed for divorce on 7 November 2006. Soon after, in early 2007, her behaviour became bizarre, sparking a series of damaging news stories, and she was admitted to a psychiatric hospital for a short spell in January 2008. In February 2009, she began her professional comeback.

(i) Looking at her chart, can you see any astrological reason for such an emphasis on so many significant personal events in her life (her second marriage and the birth of her two sons) taking place during Septembers of different years?

(ii) Looking at the transits to her chart at the time, what do you think triggered her difficulties and caused what appeared to be a nervous breakdown in January 2008?

(iii) Does her chart explain her massive worldwide fame as a singer and tabloid fodder? If so, where and how?

Question 91 • Since first appearing in *ER* in 1994, actor George Clooney has rarely been out of the headlines – not only for his looks and roles but also for his Democrat political sympathies. He appears to be that rare beast: a world-famous Hollywood star who is interested in a lot more than the size of his Winnebago and the efficiency of his hair gel.

(i) One of his friends described him as 'a grown-up man with a kid's heart'. Where can you see this in Clooney's chart?

(ii) After his marriage failed in 1992, George vowed never to get married again. A subsequent relationship foundered through Clooney's lack of commitment. (Some people have said that his deepest relationship was with his Vietnamese pot-bellied pig, Max, who died in 2006.) Where in his birth chart can you see this reluctance to become committed to another person?

(iii) Although he has acted in and directed several films with a serious political message, he is probably best loved for the wacky comedies in which he's appeared. Where can you see the 'funny man' in his horoscope?

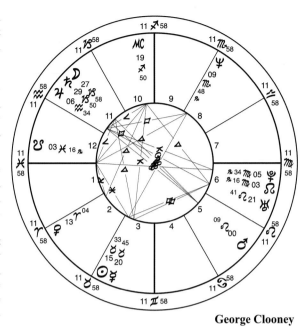

George Clooney

Question 92 • After turning pro in 1996, Tiger Woods soon made his mark on the golfing world, breaking records and amassing a fortune in the process. But his squeaky-clean image became tarnished in November 2009 because of revelations about his numerous infidelities that followed a bizarre incident involving his car, a fire hydrant and his wife.

(i) Where can you see his golfing prowess in his chart? Before answering this question, you might find it useful to

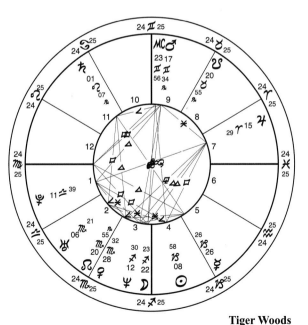

Tiger Woods

consider what you think the sport of golf requires, such as hand-eye co-ordination, patience and stamina (and possibly the ability to wear hideously patterned clothes while keeping a straight face).

(ii) It has been revealed that Tiger Woods had been making the most of the many women who threw themselves at him over the years. Where in his chart can you see his potential to be a serial philanderer?

(iii) The revelations about his private life and his infidelity were first made public in late November 2009, and soon after he announced that he was taking an indefinite break from golf in order to mend his marriage. What was happening in his chart at the time by transit?

Question 93 • Together with her older sister Venus, Serena Williams has been one of tennis's biggest stories since she first came to prominence in 1999. Since then, she has won all four Grand Slam titles. She has other interests too, particularly fashion.

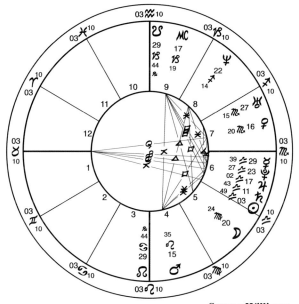

Serena Williams

(i) Serena is best friends with her sister, Venus, yet they are also professional rivals. Where can you see this close relationship?

(ii) Like her siblings, Serena was groomed from the age of four by her father to become a professional tennis player. He also home-schooled Serena and Venus. Where is his influence shown in Serena's chart?

(iii) She has a packed 6th house. Can you unravel it?

(iv) On 13 September 2009, Serena let rip at a line judge during the US Open at Flushing Meadow, New York. Her expletive-ridden rant earned her a record fine of $82,000. Looking at her transits at the time, can you see what might have triggered this outburst?

Question 94 • When President John F Kennedy was assassinated in Dallas on 22 November 1963, Lee Harvey Oswald was arrested and charged with his murder. Kennedy was driving in a motorcade when he was shot in the head and neck, whether or not by Oswald. Oswald's case never came to trial because he was shot two days later while

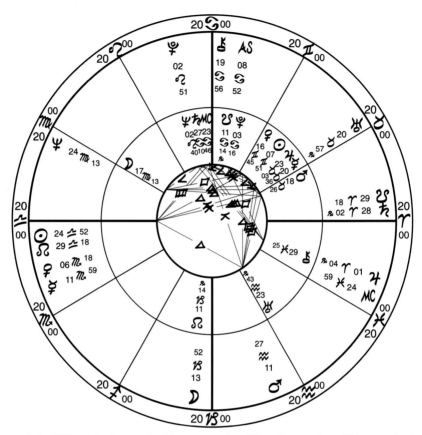

John F Kennedy (inner wheel/house cusps) and **Lee Harvey Oswald** (outer wheel)

being moved from the police headquarters to the county jail. Ever since, there has been heated debate about whether Oswald was guilty or if he was the only gunman involved.

Oswald had a difficult life. As a teenager, he was diagnosed as being emotionally disturbed, although his mother refused to give permission for his treatment. After becoming a Marxist, he defected to the USSR, where he met his wife. They returned to the US with their daughter in June 1962.

This chart shows the synastry between Kennedy (inner wheel) and Oswald (outer wheel). They never met (as far as we know) but history will always link them.

(i) Using orbs of no more than five degrees, list the links between their two charts. What do they reveal?

(ii) Can you see a description of a lone gunman shooting JFK? Can you see a description of the controversy that still surrounds this incident?

Question 95 • In her day, Greta Garbo was one of the world's most celebrated actresses. She made her last film when she was 36 and spent the rest of her life (she died at the age of 84) living in very secluded and allegedly rather strange retirement.

(i) Despite being world-famous, she shunned the limelight. One of her most iconic – and prophetic – lines was 'I want to be alone' from the film *Grand Hotel*. Where in her horoscope can you see evidence of her modesty, reticence and almost pathological desire for privacy?

(ii) Where can you see her status as one of the most iconic figures of the 20th century? What would suggest her enigmatic presence on screen?

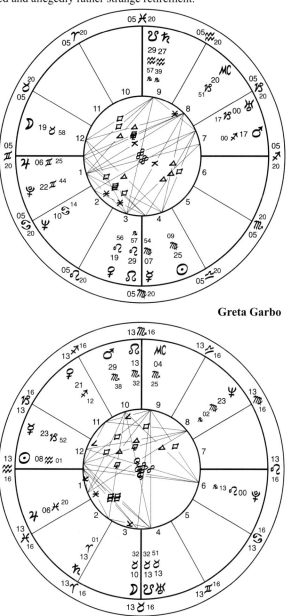

Greta Garbo

Question 96 • Germaine Greer is an Australian writer, academic and journalist who shoots from the hip and is no stranger to controversy. She hit the headlines in 1970 with the publication of her feminist book *The Female Eunuch*, and has continued to occupy an influential role ever since. Her formidable intellect means she often makes mincemeat of her detractors.

(i) She has a triple conjunction of the Moon, South Node and Uranus in Taurus

Germaine Greer

in her 4th house. How do you think this has influenced her behaviour, both privately and publicly?

(ii) Known for decades as an anarchist and a Marxist, where can you see this iconoclastic, rebellious and highly controversial side of Greer's nature? What early experiences, in your opinion, may have triggered these traits?

(iii) Until her retirement, Germaine Greer held various academic posts at British universities. Where is her academic career shown in her chart?

Question 97 • On the night of 14 April 1912, the RMS Titanic struck an iceberg as she sailed through the icy waters off Newfoundland. It was her maiden voyage and she carried fewer lifeboats than the number of her passengers warranted because she was publicized as being unsinkable. Her designers claimed that she could survive any damage that she sustained to her hull.

That evening her officers had ignored radio warnings about the presence of icebergs in their vicinity, only realizing their folly too

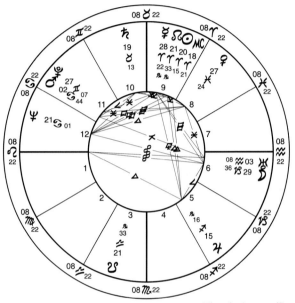

Titanic (sets sail)

late. They tried to steer the Titanic around a gigantic iceberg that loomed up at them but couldn't manage it. The iceberg ripped a hole in the Titanic's side at 23.40 (local time) and she began to take in water almost immediately. Some passengers felt the collision and hurried on deck to see what was wrong. Others were unaware of the problem.

The limited number of lifeboats soon filled up with women and children. Men were not allowed to join them. Although the Titanic's radio crew repeatedly radioed for help, no ships arrived in time. She sank less than three hours later, at 02.20, with massive loss of life: 2227 passengers and crew were on board at the time of the collision but only 705 people survived to tell the tale.

(i) In this chart for the moment when she set sail in Southampton, where can you see the claim that the Titanic was unsinkable? (There is more than one significator.)

(ii) What is the significator of the iceberg that the crew didn't expect to encounter?

(iii) Where can you see the significators that say it was her maiden voyage?

(iv) What's the significance of Mercury retrograde in Aries?

Question 98 • On the morning of 7 November 2000, a gang of criminals used a stolen mechanical digger to break into the Millennium Dome in east London and steal the massive Millennium Star diamond on display there worth £20 million, plus other valuable diamonds that were being shown in a De Beers exhibition. Little did they know that the Metropolitan Police were aware of the plan, which they had codenamed Operation Magician, and were waiting. The jewels were removed from the Dome the night before and replaced with fakes. The police were positioned around the Dome, disguised as employees, with more police stationed outside. Five men were arrested.

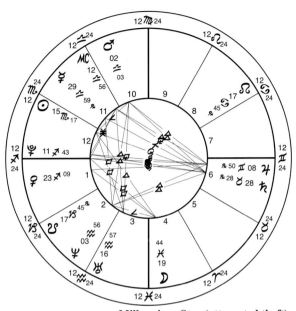

Millennium Star (attempted theft)

(i) Does the chart tell the story of the abortive raid? Describe it, giving significators.

(ii) Where can you see the priceless diamonds in this chart?

(iii) What do you think is indicated by the Libra MC and its ruler?

Question 99 • At 11.15 on the morning of 3 September 1939, people switching on their radios in Britain heard the Prime Minister, Neville Chamberlain, announce 'This morning the British Ambassador in Berlin handed the German government a final note stating that, unless we heard from them by 11 o'clock that they were prepared at once to withdraw their troops from Poland, a state of war would exist between us. I have to tell you now that no such undertaking has been received, and that consequently this country is at war with Germany.'

Over the page is the horoscope for the start of the war between Britain, France and Germany, set for Westminster. The war raged around the world for six years, involving almost every country on the face of the planet and killing approximately 50 million people.

(i) What are the chart features that strike you immediately?

(ii) Where can you see its description of an event or decision that would turn into a global war?

(iii) What is your interpretation of the grand trine in Earth between Mars, Neptune and Uranus?

(iv) What do you make of the very close Saturn and Moon opposition to the North Node stretched across the Ascendant/Descendant axis?

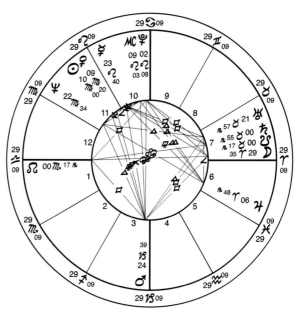

Britain Declares War

Question 100 • Here is the chart of a woman whose work was celebrated during and after her life. Using all the experience you've gained while working your way through this book, what can you deduce about her? What were the main themes and drives of her life?

What does the chart tell you about her personality, with its strengths and weaknesses? Can you find any clues about what she did for a living? What was the impact she had on the world, both in her relationships and in her professional life? What was her home life like? Give the astrological significators for each of your findings.

Question 101 • One final question – about you. Where do you see an interest in astrology in your own chart? And what sort of astrologer do you think you'll make?

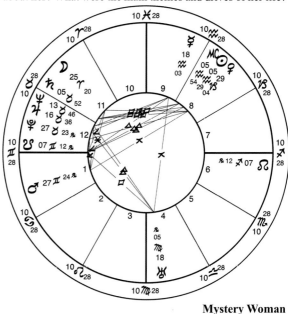

Mystery Woman